PIANO SOLO

THE HUNGER GAMES
MUSIC FROM THE MOTION PICTURE SCORE

2   KATNISS AFOOT

5   REAPING DAY

18 THE TRAIN

6   PREPARING THE CHARIOTS

8   HORN OF PLENTY

12 THE COUNTDOWN

14 HEALING KATNISS

19 SEARCHING FOR PEETA

22 THE CAVE

24 RETURNING HOME

ISBN 978-1-4768-0531-3

7777 W. BLUEMOUND RD. P.O. BOX 13819 MILWAUKEE, WI 53213

Visit Hal Leonard Online at
www.halleonard.com

KATNISS AFOOT

By JAMES NEWTON HOWARD

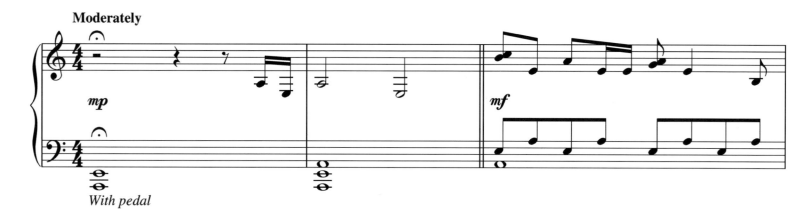

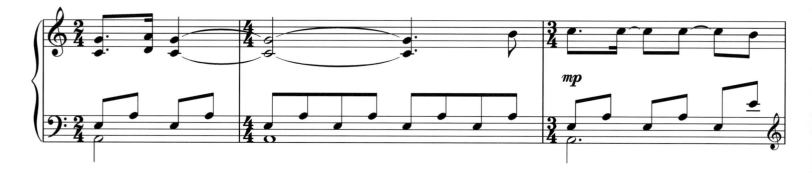

REAPING DAY

By JAMES NEWTON HOWARD

PREPARING THE CHARIOTS

By JAMES NEWTON HOWARD

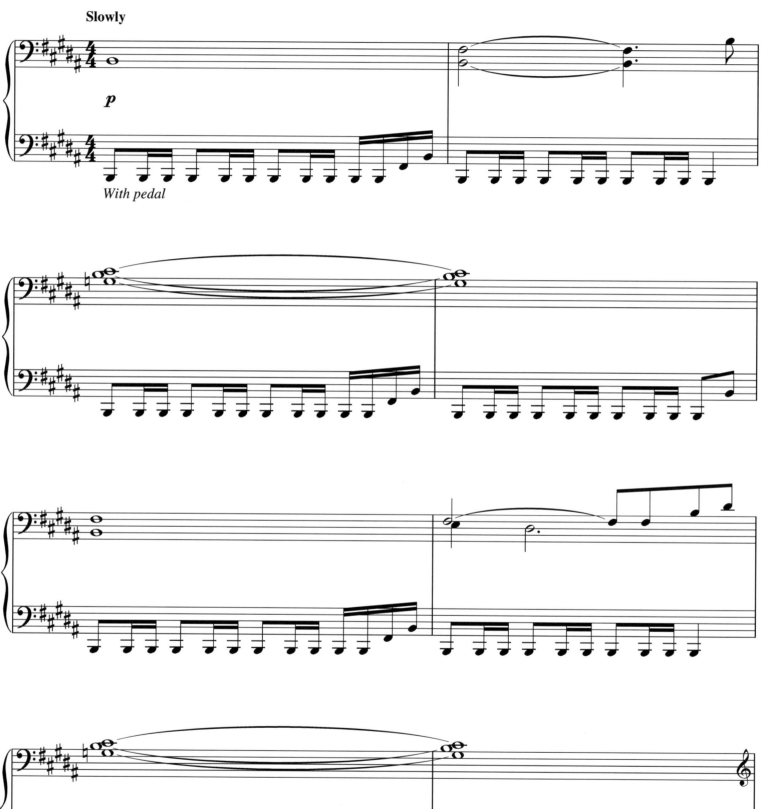

Segue to "Horn of Plenty"

HORN OF PLENTY

By WIN BUTLER and REGINE CHASSAGNE

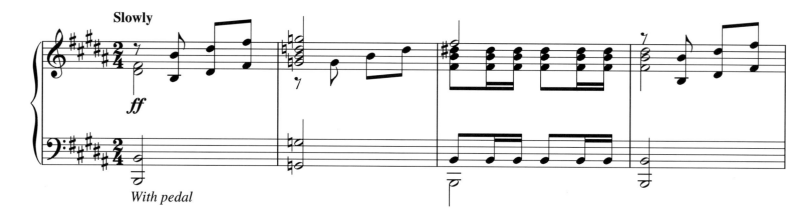

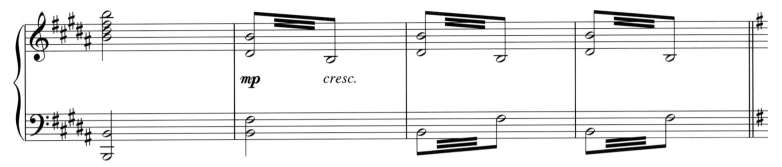

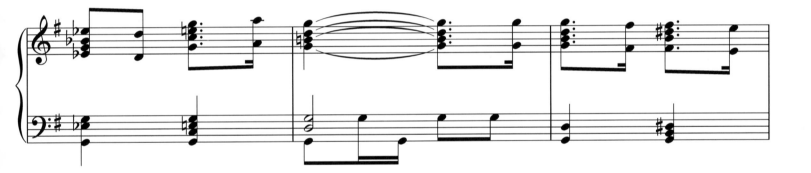

THE COUNTDOWN

By JAMES NEWTON HOWARD

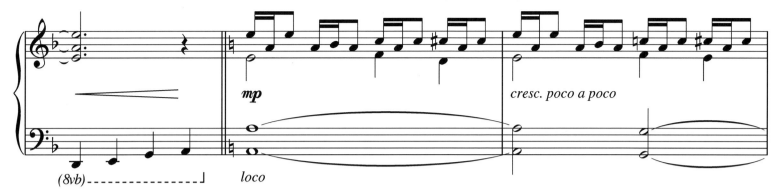

HEALING KATNISS

By JAMES NEWTON HOWARD

Moderately fast

mp

With pedal

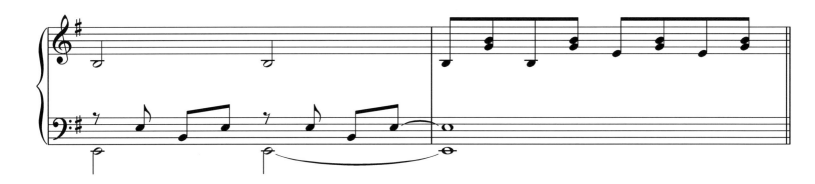

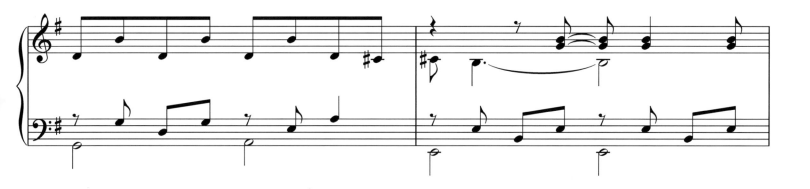

THE TRAIN

By JAMES NEWTON HOWARD

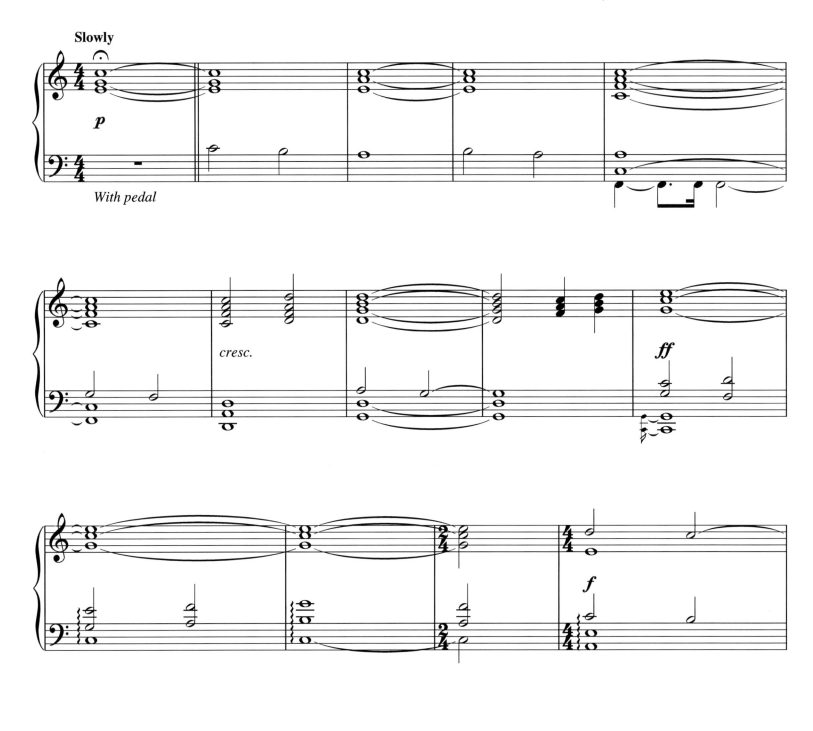

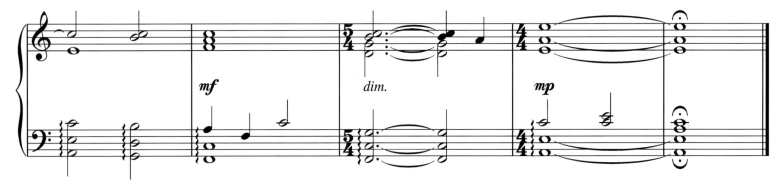

SEARCHING FOR PEETA

By JAMES NEWTON HOWARD

Moderately slow

With pedal

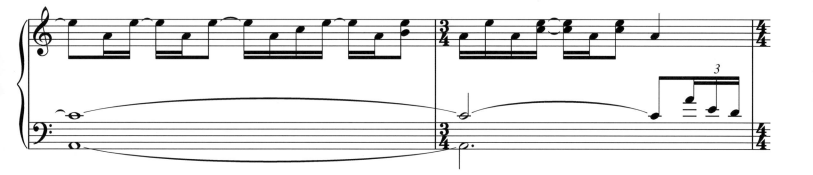

Very slowly

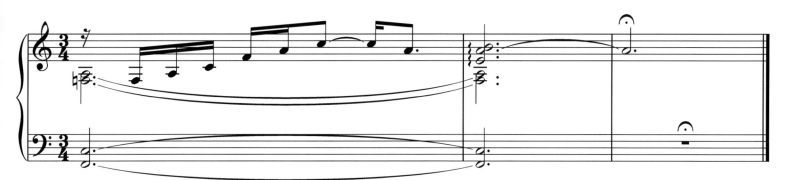

THE CAVE

By JAMES NEWTON HOWARD

Slowly

With pedal

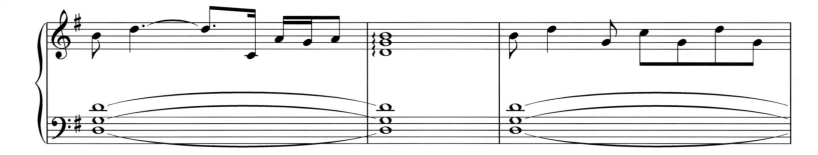

RETURNING HOME

By JAMES NEWTON HOWARD

Slowly and expressively